COLOR

&

Learn Portuguese With Girrafe Easy Italian For Kids

By Gogo dada Coloring books

Copyright © 2020
All rights reserved,
No part of this publication may be reproduced, distributed, or transmitted in any form or by any means, including photocopying, recording, or other electronic or mechanical methods, without the prior written permission of the publisher, except in the case of brief quotations embodied in critical reviews and certain other noncommercial uses permitted by copyright law

By Gogo dada Coloring books

Hello

How are you?

I'm Good

What's your name?

Nice to meet you too Good Bye!

A B C IN Portuguese (Alfabeto)

Avião
(Airplane)

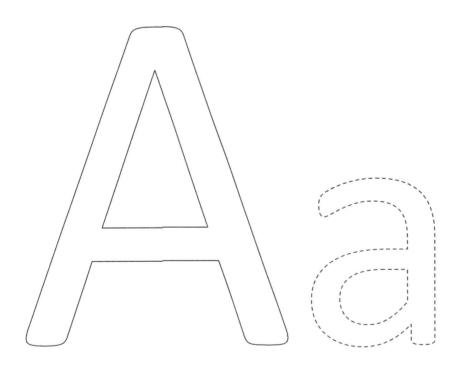

Barco
(Boat)

B b

Circo
(Circus)

Cc

Dinossauro
(Dinosaur)

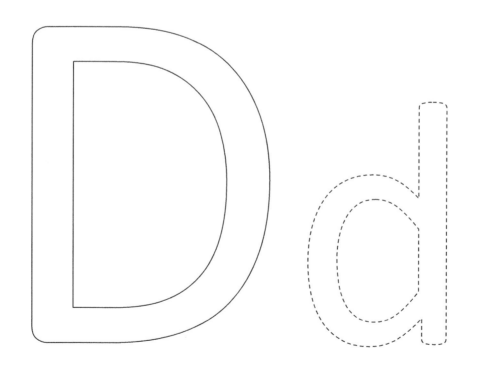

Elefante
(Elephant)

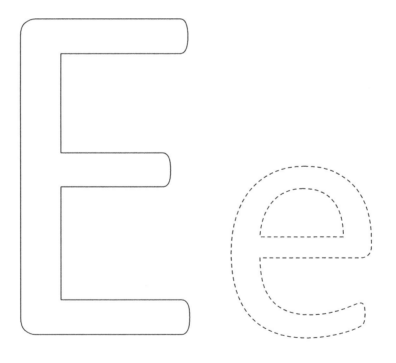

Flor
(Flower)

F f

Girafa
(Giraffe)

Gg

Helicóptero
(Helicopter)

H h

Igloo
(Iglu)

Ii

Leão
(Lion)

L l

Motocicleta
(Motorcycle)

M m

Night
(Noite)

N n

Ocean
(Oceano)

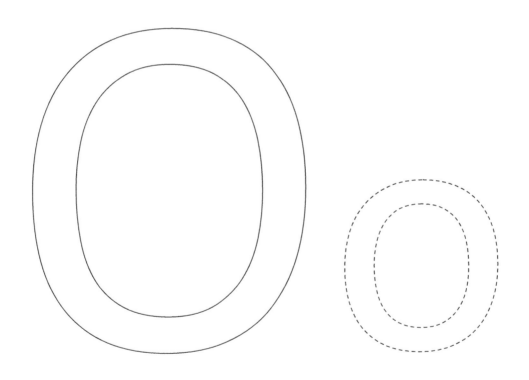

Pera
(Papagaio)

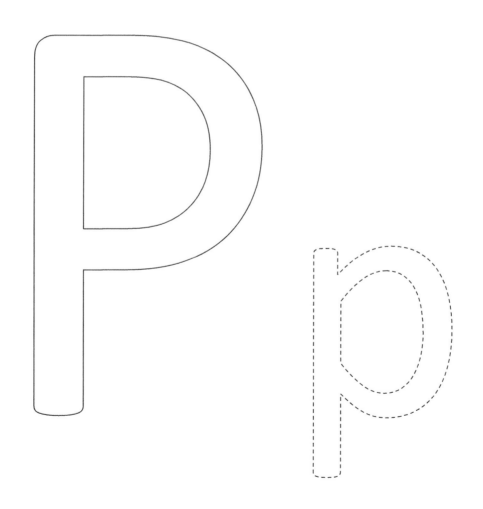

Quiche
(Quiche)

Rato
(Rat)

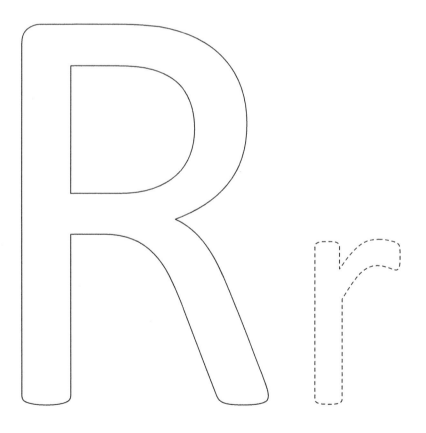

Snake
(Serpente)

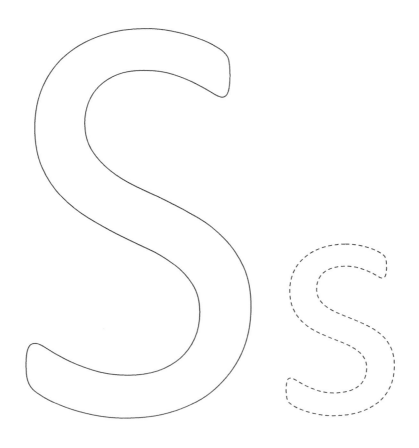

Tigre
(Tiger)

T t

Unicórnio
(Unicorn)

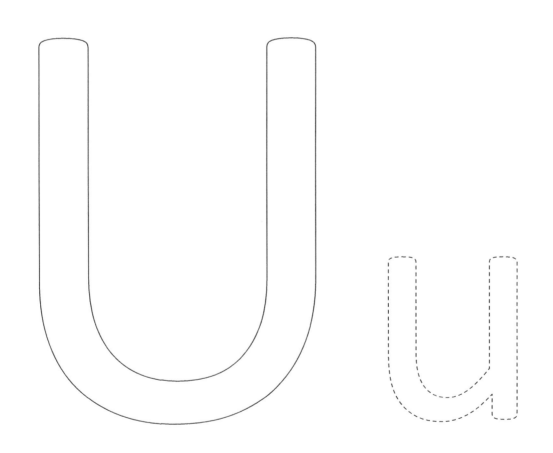

Volcano
(Vulcão)

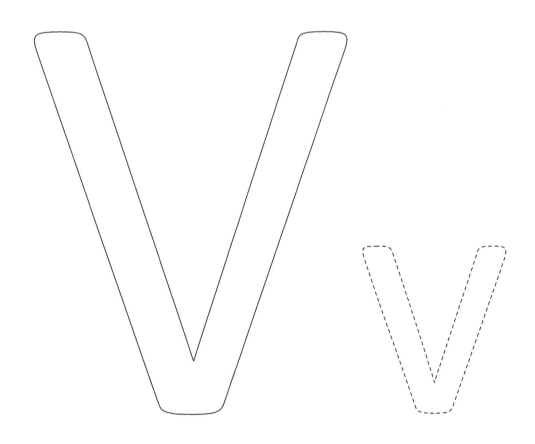

Wi-Fi

(Wi-Fi)

W w

Xilofone
(Xylophone)

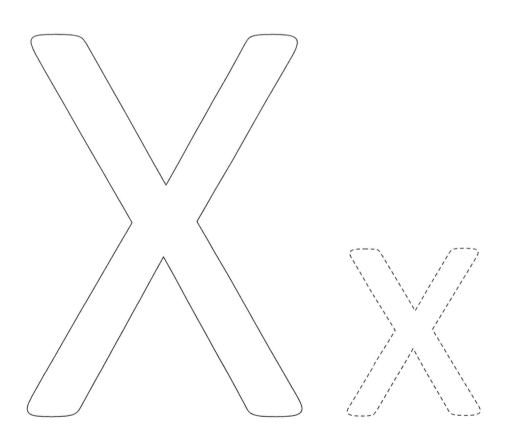

Yeti
(Yeti)

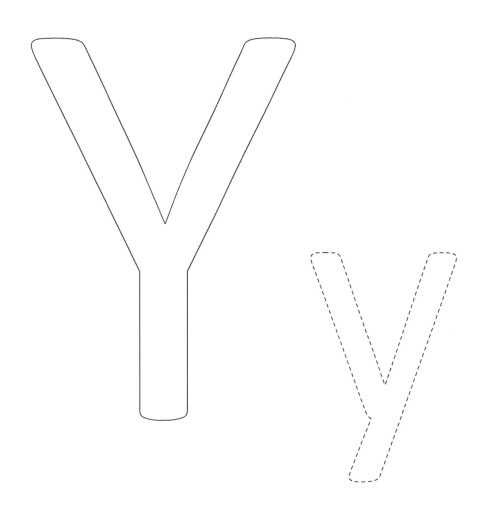

Zebra
(Zebra)

Zz

Let's Move on To the Numbers 0 To 20

Zero

0

Zero

1 Um

One

3 Três

Three

4 Quatro

Four

5 Cinco

Five

6 Seis

Six

7 Sete

Seven

8 Oito

Eight

9 Nove

nine

10 Dez

Ten

11 Onze

Eleven

12 Doze

Twelve

13 Treze

Thirteen

14 Quatorze

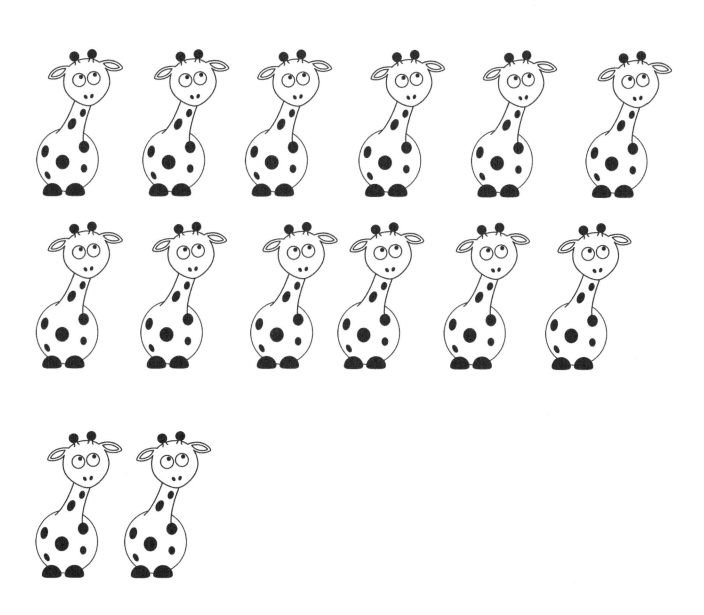

Fourteen

15 Quinze

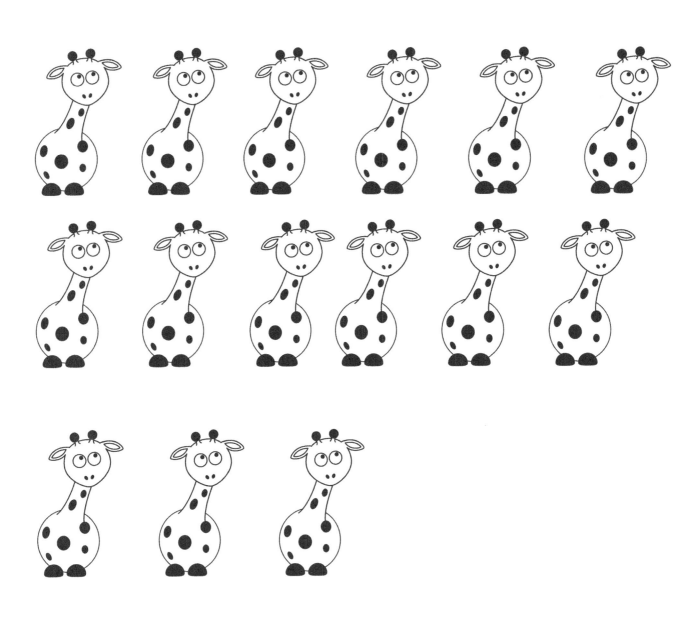

FIFTEEN

16 Dezesseis

Sixteen

17 Dezessete

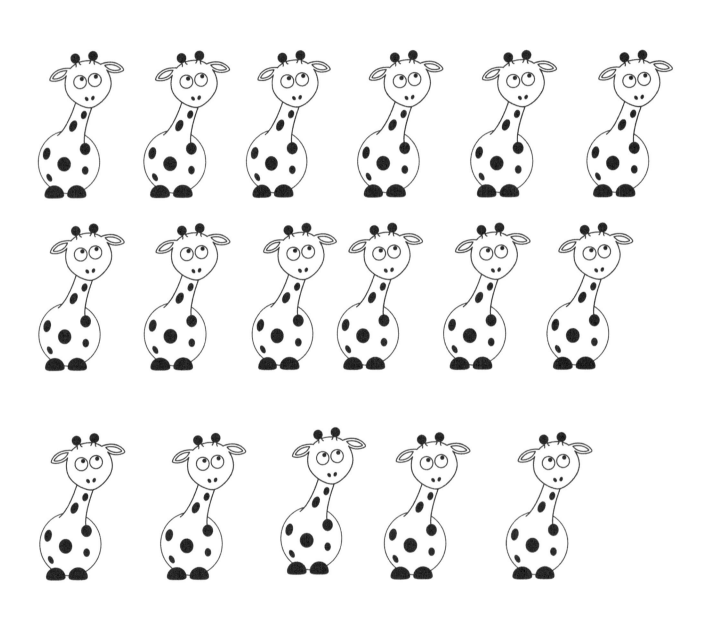

Seventeen

18 Dezoito

Eighteen

19 Dezenove

nineteen

20 Vinte

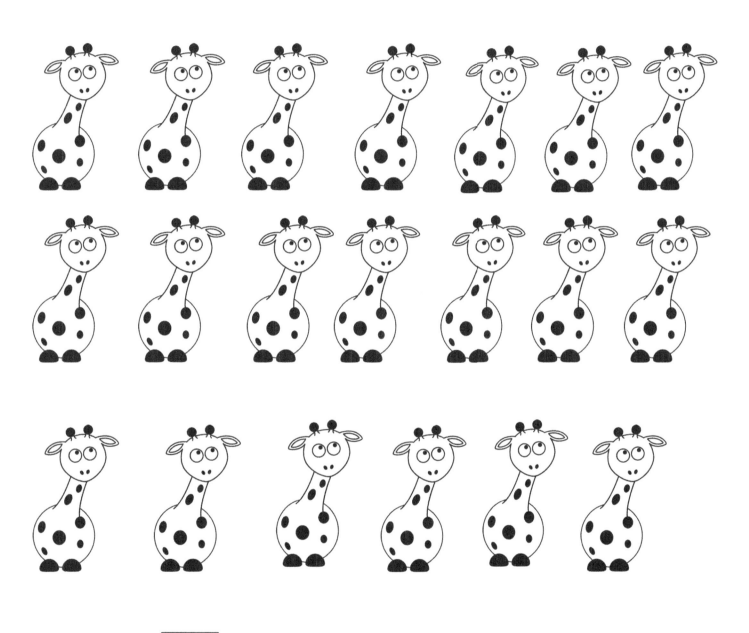

Twenty

1+0= 1 Um

1+1= 2 Dois

1+2= 3 Três

1+3= 4

1 2 3 4 quatro

Days of the Week In Portuguese

Segunda-feira

Monday

Terça-feira

Tuesday

Quarta-feira

Wednesday

Quinta-feira

Thursday

Sábado

Saturday

Months of the year In Portuguese

Janeiro

1

January

Fevereiro

2

February

Março

3

March

Abril

4

April

Maio

5

May

Junho

6

June

Julho

7

July

Agosto

8

August

Setembro

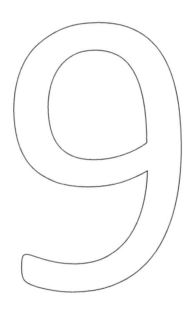

September

Outubro

10

October

Novembro

11

November

Dezembro

12

December

The Four Seasons Of The Year In Portuguese

Primavera

Spring

Outono

Autumn

Inverno

Winter

Made in the USA
Middletown, DE
09 May 2021